CATHERINE THE GREAT

A Life From Beginning to End

Copyright © 2017 by Hourly History.

Table of Contents

Introduction

The eighteenth century in Russia was a period of change considered by historians to be the Russian Age of Enlightenment. During this time, Russian leaders actively encouraged the proliferation of arts and sciences, and toward that end, the first Russian university was founded as well as a library, a theatre, a museum, and a relatively independent press. The Enlightenment in Russia differed somewhat from that of western Europe in that modernization was encouraged in all aspects of Russian life, and there was also a push to abolish the institution of serfdom.

Many of the ideas associated with the Russian Enlightenment were first espoused during the reign of Peter the Great, who ruled from 1721 to 1725. It was during his reign that a cultural revolution occurred, resulting in the replacement of traditionalist social and political systems with more modern, scientific, westernized systems based on the Enlightenment in Europe. Peter's daughter, Elizabeth Petrovna, who ruled between 1741 and 1762, introduced the concept of enlightened absolutism, also known as enlightened despotism. Enlightened despotism was a form of absolute monarchy in which the monarchs embraced rationality, fostered education, promoted religious tolerance and freedom of speech, and believed in the right to hold private property. The concept derived from an essay written by the Prussian ruler Frederick the Great, but it was Elizabeth who introduced the idea to Russia.

One of the most influential rulers during the Russian Enlightenment, however, was Catherine the Great. Catherine the Great was born Princess Sophie of Anhalt-Zerbst. She was the longest-ruling female in Russian history. She ruled from July 1762 to November 1796, during what has been called the Catherinian Era. The time of her rule is considered the Golden Age of the Russian Empire. During her rule, she sought to modernize Russia, bringing it up to par militarily, politically, culturally, and intellectually with its neighbors. She succeeded in achieving many of her goals, and for this, she is considered one of the most renowned leaders in Russian history.

Chapter One

The Early Life of an Empress

"A great wind is blowing, and that gives you either imagination or a headache."

—Catherine the Great

Catherine the Great was born in Prussia in Stettin, Pomerania on May 2, 1729. She was born Sophie Friederike Auguste von Anhalt-Zerbst-Dornburg to Christian August, Prince of Anhalt-Zerbst, and Johanna Elisabeth of Holstein-Gottorp. Though he was a prince, her father held the rank of a general in his capacity as governor of Stettin (modern-day Szczecin, Poland). Catherine's extended family were part of the ruling class as well. Two of her cousins became kings of Sweden— Gustav III and Charles XIII. Though part of the ruling class, her family had little money, and it was wealthy relatives on her mother's side who would support her rise to power. Catherine's potential for becoming empress of Russia was something her mother Johanna was focused on, so much so that her meddling got her banned from Russia for spying on King Frederick of Prussia.

Because she was part of the ruling class, as was customary, Catherine was educated by a French governess and tutors. Of her childhood, she later wrote that she saw "nothing of interest in it." It was relatively uneventful. As she grew to womanhood, a number of powerful interests took part in arranging her marriage to a prospective tsar, Peter of Holstein-Gottorp. Even Frederick II of Prussia and the Russian Empress Elizabeth were involved in the diplomacy of arranging the union. Count Jean Armand de L'Estocq, a French adventurer with considerable influence on the Russian empress, also played a role.

Catherine's marriage to Peter was arranged in order to strengthen the friendship between Prussia and Russia, and consequently weaken Austria's influence on Russia. Additionally, for Frederick and L'Estocq, the goal was to ruin the Russian chancellor Bestuzhev, who was a supporter of Russo-Austrian cooperation and a confidante of Empress Elizabeth. For her part, Catherine first met Peter at age ten, and she detested him. She stated that she disliked his pale complexion, his drinking, and the fact that he still played with toy soldiers. She would later write that she and Peter resided on opposite ends of the castle from one another.

Though she detested Peter, Catherine loved Russia, and despite the unwanted interference of her mother who infuriated Empress Elizabeth with her meddling, Elizabeth liked Catherine. Upon arriving in Russia, Catherine did everything she could to ingratiate herself with the empress, her husband, and the Russian people. Her efforts included learning the Russian language and converting from Lutheran to Eastern Orthodoxy. She is said to have taken her lessons in the Russian language so seriously that she would rise at night and walk around her room repeating what she had learned.

She did eventually master the language, but her zeal led to a bout of pneumonia in March 1744. She was treated by bloodletting, and she credited that with saving her life. Though Catherine saw the practice as her savior, her mother was opposed to the method. When Catherine was in the throes of delirium, her mother wanted her confessed by a Lutheran priest, but upon waking, Catherine is said to have proclaimed that she didn't want that, but instead wanted her Orthodox father. The empress was very impressed by this, and Catherine gained esteem in her eyes.

Her conversion to Eastern Orthodoxy was something her father, a devout Lutheran, opposed, but Catherine, who at that time was still named Sophie, persisted. She was determined to do everything it took in order to become qualified to rule the country. In June 1744, she was accepted as a member of the Russian Orthodox Church, and as such, she was given a new name— Catherine, daughter of Aleksey. The day after she was welcomed into the church, she became formally betrothed to Peter. They were married on August 21, 1745, in St. Petersburg. Catherine was just 16 years old, and her father refused to attend the wedding. At the time of the ceremony, Catherine's husband, Peter von Holstein- Gottorp, had become the Duke of Holstein-Gottorp, which was located in the northwest of modern Germany near the border of Denmark.

After their marriage, Peter and Catherine settled in Oranienbaum. They held court there for many years. Catherine did not come to love Peter; rather rumors abounded at the time that Peter had taken a mistress, and Catherine had liaisons with several lovers. Catherine also became friends with the sister of her husband's mistress, Princess Yekaterina Vorontsova-Dashkova, who introduced her to various political groups opposing her husband.

Peter's behavior became increasingly unbearable for those living in the palace. When Catherine's second child, Anna, died at only four months of age, Peter, who believed the child was not his, is said to have proclaimed, "Go to the Devil!" after Catherine dismissed his accusations. Because of his moodiness, Catherine increasingly hid away in her private boudoir to avoid his abrasive personality. Though secluded, Catherine remained optimistic, stating in her memoirs, "If you feel unhappy, raise yourself above unhappiness, and so act that your happiness may be independent of all eventualities."

Empress Elizabeth died on January 5, 1762, and Peter succeeded to the throne. He became Emperor Peter III, and Catherine became empress consort, which is what the wives of Russian emperors were called. At that time, the couple moved to the Winter Palace in St. Petersburg. As tsar, Peter III had many eccentricities and policies that Catherine, and the groups that Catherine had cultivated, opposed. He had a great admiration for Frederick II, King of Prussia, with whom Russia had fought from 1756 to

1763 in a conflict known as the Seven Years' War. The newly crowned tsar supported Frederick II's suggestion to partition Polish territories with Russia. This was something the Russian nobility opposed. Thus, Peter had set the stage for what was about to happen.

In July 1762, a mere six months after becoming emperor, Peter and his Holstein-born courtiers and relatives went on holiday to Oranienbaum. Staying behind in St. Petersburg, Catherine had been conspiring with opponents of her husband to seize the throne. After Peter left for Oranienbaum, Catherine learned that one of her co-conspirators had been arrested. Given this development, she and her supporters knew they had to act fast. She departed for the Izmailovsky Regiment, which was one of the oldest regiments in the Russian army, where she gave a speech requesting that the unit protect her from her husband. They agreed, and Catherine then went to the Semenovsky Barracks where the clergy was waiting to ordain her as the sole occupant of the throne. Following these successes, Catherine then had her husband arrested after which she forced him to sign a document abdicating the throne. With his abdication, there was no one to oppose her. Six months later, Peter died at the hands of Alexei Orlov who was the younger brother of Grigory Orlov. Grigory had participated in the coup. Historians can find no evidence that Catherine was complicit in the assassination; however, it was a convenient coincidence.

There were other claimants to the throne after Peter was deposed. Ivan VI had been kept in solitary confinement from the age of six months (he was born in 1740), but he was also assassinated in 1764 after an attempt to free him as part of a coup against Catherine. This time, there was no doubt Catherine had played a role in his death. Catherine, like Empress Elizabeth before her, had left strict instructions that he should be killed in the event of a coup attempt against her. Though some questioned Catherine's right to rule, she was following the precedent set by Catherine I, who had been born to lower classes in the Swedish Baltic territories, when she succeeded her husband, Peter the Great, in 1725. She, too, had the guard regiments declare her the new empress.

Despite the precedent set by Catherine I, many historians still debate Catherine the Great's status. Though she was declared empress regnant, which means the new empress with full rights to rule, many historians still see her as empress regent, ruling only until her son, Grand Duke Paul, was old enough to take over. In fact, in the 1770s, nobles who were connected with her son considered a coup to transfer the crown to him, but nothing ever came of that idea. So it was that, on June 28, 1762, Catherine rallied the regiments to St. Petersburg where she then declared herself Catherine II, the sovereign ruler of Russia. Her son Paul was named as her legitimate heir.

Chapter Two

The Dawn of a New Era

"In politics, a capable leader must be guided by circumstances, conjectures, and conjunctions."

—Catherine the Great

Catherine was formally crowned on September 22, 1762, at the Assumption Cathedral in Moscow. She assumed the throne with the assistance of her lover, Grigory Orlov. For her coronation, what has become one of the main treasures of the Romanov Dynasty, the Imperial Crown of Russia was created. It was constructed of two gold and silver half spheres, which represented the eastern and western Roman empires, and contained 75 pearls, 4,936 Indian diamonds, and a 398.62-carat ruby spinel, which previously belonged to Empress Elizabeth. It also included a diamond cross. Weighing in at a little over five pounds (2.3 kg), the piece was designed by Jérémie Pauzié, a Swiss-French court diamond jeweler. The design was inspired by crowns of the Byzantine Empire. The crown would become the coronation crown for Romanov emperors from that point forward. After the death of Tsar Nicholas II in 1918, it became a treasure of the Romanov Dynasty and is now housed at the Moscow Kremlin Armoury Museum.

For Catherine, ruling Russia was what she had spent her life preparing for, and she knew what she wanted to do. Above all else, she sought to modernize Russia on a par with what was happening in Europe. To begin with, the Russian economy was well below the standards in western Europe. Russia did not have a free peasantry, a significant middle class, nor laws amenable to private enterprise. There were some textile industries around Moscow, and there was an ironworks in the Ural Mountains, but the latter was supported mainly by serf labor. Serfs were not exactly slaves, but they weren't quite indentured servants either. They didn't have many rights, but they could accumulate wealth and purchase their freedom.

To modernize the Russian economy, Catherine encouraged the immigration of German farmers into the Volga River Valley. They brought with them many innovations that were ultimately responsible for modernizing the sector. This included the modernization of wheat production, flour milling, the tobacco industry, sheep raising, and small-scale manufacturing. With the help of these immigrants, the region rose to dominate the Russian economy.

In addition to her immigration policy, Catherine oversaw the issuance of the first government paper money, a task she assigned to the Assignation Bank, which opened in St. Petersburg and Moscow in 1769. After those initial openings, several branches were later established in smaller towns, which were referred to as government towns. The bank issued paper notes following payment of similar sums in copper money. The copper coins could also be refunded by presenting the paper notes. The paper notes were called Assignation rubles, and they became necessary due to the large amount of government spending for military needs combined with a shortage of silver in the treasury. The shortage had occurred as a result of the military spending, but also as a consequence of an increase in foreign trade, which was conducted almost exclusively in silver and gold coins. The use of the notes continued until 1849.

Another prong in Catherine's goal of modernizing Russia was the modernization of the educational system. Catherine believed that Russians could be turned away from the backward-thinking that was typical of the time if they were properly educated. For Catherine, this meant inculcating Russian children with European education. The European system sought to develop students both intellectually and morally, providing them with the proper knowledge and skills and promoting a sense of civic duty.

Ivan Betskoy was appointed as Catherine's educational advisor. He collected and presented to her information about educational institutions in Russia as opposed to those in other countries. Catherine then established an educational commission and consulted with educational pioneers in Britain, such as the Reverend Daniel Dumaresq and Dr. John Brown. In fact, she had Dumaresq come to Russia where she appointed him to her educational commission. She tasked the commission with studying various educational systems in order to establish a general education system for all Russian Orthodox subjects between the ages of 5 and 18 years.

Catherine emphasized the proper education of both sexes, something also advocated by Dr. John Brown. Toward that end, Catherine had experimented with this concept as well as new educational theories after establishing the Moscow Foundling Home, which was charged with admitting destitute and extramarital children and educating them in the manner the state deemed proper. It failed because of high mortality rates, but not long after that, Catherine established the Smolny Institute for Noble Girls. This was the first of its kind in Russia and was tasked specifically with educating females. While at first it only admitted the children of nobility, it later admitted girls of the bourgeoisie. At the institute, the children were taught French, musicianship, dancing, and complete awe of the monarch. Central to the philosophy of the institute was discipline. As a result, running and games of any kind were forbidden. Excess play was considered harmful to developing bodies as was too much warmth. Thus, the building was kept at a very cold temperature.

All of this was ongoing as the commission made little progress in its efforts to help establish a national school system. Catherine persisted in that effort though, and she succeeded in making numerous reforms. She remodeled the Cadet Corps 1766, which subsequently began educating children from a very young age until they were 21 years old. The curriculum was broadened to include sciences, philosophy, ethics, history, and international law as well as the professional military curriculum it taught previously. This policy also influenced that of the Naval Cadet Corps and the Engineering and Artillery Schools.

In 1782, Catherine again established an advisory commission tasked with gathering more information about educational systems used in other countries. She was particularly impressed by an Austrian system produced by mathematician Franz Aepinus, who favored a three-tier model at the village, town, and provincial capital levels. With this system in mind, Catherine established a Commission of National Schools under the leadership of Pyotr Zavadovsky. Zavadovsky was charged with organizing a national school system, training teachers, and providing textbooks. From this effort, the Russian Statute of National Education was created on August 5, 1786. The statute produced a two-tier system of primary schools and high schools that were free, open to children of any class with the exception of serfs. The statute strictly regulated all of the school subjects as well as the methods of teaching. The commission also translated textbooks and provided teachers with a guide that dealt with teaching methods, subjects, the behavior of the teacher, and how to run the school.

Though the effort to reform the educational system was considerable, the criticism of it was harsh. Critics claimed that Catherine failed to supply enough money to the educational programs, and two years after it was implemented, inspectors encountered a tepid response from the nobility, who still preferred to send their children to private, more prestigious institutions. They also found that the townspeople rebelled against the pedagogical methods of the junior schools. Thus, near the end of Catherine's reign, only about 62,000 pupils were being educated in approximately 549 state institutions. That number represents a small amount of people as compared to the size of the Russian population at the time.

While Catherine's efforts at educational reform were heavily criticized, she did build upon the efforts of Peter the Great in seeking to broaden and modernize the Russian system. Her downfall, many argue, was in her embrace of enlightened absolutism, which argued against the education of the peasantry. Catherine wrote in a letter to her associates, "Plebeians should not be educated, otherwise they will know as much as you and I and will not obey us to the same extent as now." Because of this attitude, she failed to provide funds to establish adequate schools for peasants and train teachers to educate them. Many historians argue this minimized her success in reforming the Russian educational system.

Catherine's attitude toward the peasantry was not uncommon of the times. The system of serfdom was something that had existed before Catherine's reign, and her attitude reflected that of the nobility into which she had been born. Serfs were free people of the peasant class who would give up their freedom to a landowner in exchange for protection as well as support in times of hardship. The serfs would be given land to till, but they would have to give up a certain percentage of their crops as a tax paid to the landowner. The serfs were not allowed to have possessions though they could accumulate wealth and later purchase their freedom. The laws governing serfdom in Russia were not clear and often weak at best. Thus, there was significant flexibility in practice with regard to the rights of both serfs and landowners.

While Catherine inherited the system as described, she did make some changes. She expanded the rights of serfs to include the right to file complaints against landowners to the proper authorities. Her reasons were not altogether altruistic, however, as she did it mainly so that she would not have to be bothered with their complaints. Catherine wanted to be free from their direct appeals to her, but she did not want them to revolt either. In establishing this additional right, she did grant the serfs a legitimate bureaucratic status they had lacked before, and many were now able to use that to their advantage. They could apply to be freed, for example, if they were under illegal ownership; non-nobles were not allowed to own serfs. Additionally, some governors were sympathetic to the causes of the serfs and listened to their complaints even to the extent of punishing the nobles.

While Catherine was not advocating for the serfs, she did take other measures that improved their conditions. She eliminated many ways for people to become serfs such as prohibiting a person who had been a serf and gained their freedom from becoming a serf again. On the other hand, she also took actions to restrict the freedom of peasants. For example, she gave away many state-owned farmers to landowners to become serfs. She also annulled an act by Peter the Great that had freed the serfs belonging to the Orthodox Church. The serfs, then, were very suspicious of Catherine, and they grew increasingly discontent.

After a major crop failure due to an epidemic in 1771, actions that were taken by the nobles to impose stricter rule and further limit the freedoms of the serfs resulted in widespread outbreaks of violence and rioting in 1774. This became known as Pugachev's Rebellion. Yemelyan Pugachev was a disaffected ex-lieutenant of the Russian Imperial Army who had assumed leadership of an alternative government in the name of Peter III. He claimed he should be tsar, and because he helped the common people, advocated for an end to serfdom, and acted on their behalf, many peasants rallied around him, giving rise to the violence. The rebellion was the largest peasant revolt in Russian history, but despite the government's failure to respond effectively initially, the uprising was crushed near the end of 1774, and Pugachev was captured and executed in January 1775.

Despite some improvement in their rights, the serfs remained unhappy and discontent throughout Catherine's rule. While she did slightly improve their lot in life, she did so only so she would not have to receive the petitions of the peasants who were complaining about their landowners. Her policies on this front, therefore, had little impact on daily life among the peasants. While her policies toward the economy and educational system of Russia were progressive, her conservative attitude toward the peasantry was not one the reflected modern thinking. Her attention was focused on modernizing

Russian culture, and it is here where she had more
success.

Chapter Three

A Patron of the Arts

"It is better to inspire a reform than to enforce it."

—Catherine the Great

Catherine had grand designs for reforming the culture of Russia. Along with modernization in the educational system, for which she, among other things, wrote educational manuals and established the famous Smolny Institute to educate young girls of nobility, she was also a lover of literature, painting, and philosophy, and a promoter of the ideals of the European Enlightenment. Because of this, Catherine founded the Hermitage Museum in St. Petersburg. The museum still celebrates its founding on December 7, 1764, as St. Catherine's Day. It houses, among many other items, the largest collection of paintings in the world. In receiving Elisabeth Vigée, the former court painter to Marie Antoinette, Catherine is said to have remarked, "I am very fond of the arts, especially painting. I am no connoisseur, but I am a great art lover."

That Catherine was not a connoisseur is debatable. She participated in the arts as much as appreciated them. She wrote comedies, fiction, and memoirs. For these efforts, she was lauded by the likes of Voltaire, Diderot, and d'Alembert. She was particularly fond of Voltaire, and he returned her praise, praising her accomplishments and referring to her as The Star of the North. She never met him in person, but she mourned him when he died, and she acquired his collections of books from his heirs. These were then placed in the National Library of Russia. For Diderot, when the French government threatened to stop his publication of the *Encyclopédie* because of its irreverent take on religion, she proposed that he complete his work in Russia under her protection.

Catherine, herself, was more or less indifferent to religion. While she had converted to Eastern Orthodoxy while seeking the crown, as ruler, she nationalized all of the church lands to pay for wars. She also mostly emptied the monasteries and required the remaining clergy to work as farmers or charge for their services in order to survive. The church became less important as the nobility, very few of whom joined the church, gained in prestige and power. Religious dissenters were not allowed to build chapels under her rule, and Catherine outright suppressed religious dissent after the start of the French Revolution.

Still, she promoted her Christian belief. She instituted a policy protecting Christians under Turkish rule, she restricted Roman Catholics in their practices, and she prohibited Muslims from owning any Orthodox serfs. She also actively pressured conversion to Orthodoxy through monetary incentives. Additionally, she had banned the Muslim pilgrimage to Mecca, the Hajj, though she later changed that after creating the Legislative Commission of 1767. This commission offered to protect the religious rights of Muslims, but public outcry was fierce. Many people burned mosques as a sign of their displeasure.

Still, Catherine chose to assimilate Islam rather than ban it, and with the Toleration of Faiths Edict of 1773, Muslims were allowed to build mosques and practice their traditions, including the Hajj. Catherine then created the Orenburg Muslim Spiritual Assembly to regulate regions with Muslim populations. The assembly was designed to regulate the instruction and ideals of the mullahs, and the positions created for this assembly were paid for by Catherine and her government. It represented a passive attempt to control both Muslims and the outer fringes of her country as well as the religious affairs of the nation.

With regard to Judaism, Catherine treated it as a separate legal and bureaucratic system. It was a small religion in Russia up until 1772. In 1772, Catherine agreed to the First Partition of Poland, which ended the existence of the Polish-Lithuanian Commonwealth by 1795. At that time, Russia incorporated a large, new Jewish population within their borders. She treated them as a separate people, defined by religion, and allowed them to separate themselves from Orthodox society, but with certain restrictions. They were taxed more, a tax which was lifted if they converted to the Orthodox faith. Additionally, Jews who converted were allowed to enter the merchant class and could then farm as free peasants under Russian rule.

Catherine began to attempt to assimilate Jews with the Charter of the Towns of 1782. She included them in the rights and laws established by the charter, and accordingly, they were recognized as equal to Orthodox citizens. Orthodox Russians disliked this for economic reasons, and they pressured Catherine to keep them away from certain economic spheres. This caused Catherine to ban Jews from Moscow's middle class in 1790. In 1794, she once again doubled the taxes on Jews and officially declared that Jews bore no relation to Russians.

While Catherine took steps during her reign to protect and promote the Orthodox Church, in many ways, it fared no better than its foreign counterparts under her rule. Catherine expropriated the church's lands and placed the control of the budget for monasteries and bishoprics under the College of Economy. There, the endowments from the government were largely replaced by income from privately held lands. Over 500 of the 954 monasteries were closed, and of the remaining, only 161 received any government money. While other religions had seats on the Legislative Commission created in 1767, the Orthodox Church did not receive even one seat. Effectively, the role of the church was severely restricted during her reign.

Catherine also had religious education strictly reviewed and called for a reform of religious schools. The latter never got past the planning stages, however, and by 1786, Catherine excluded religion from participating in the lay education system. In a Russian version of the separation of church and state, Catherine began to secularize the day-to-day operations of the state. Furthermore, although she had attempted to mend a rift with the Orthodox Church by allowing a sect called the

Old Believers to openly practice their faith, she later rescinded that tolerance when the Old Believers refused to comply with her desire to recall them into the official church, and she responded by deporting over 20,000 of them to Siberia. In her later years, she allowed them to seek election to municipal positions and promised them religious freedom if they wanted to settle again in western Russia.

At best, Catherine's attitude toward religion could be viewed as one of secularism. The frequency of her changes in attitude toward the various faiths practicing within Russia at that time demonstrates a lack of conviction. She could hardly turn her back outright on matters of faith, but she also refused to be constrained by the tenets of any one religion.

For those ideals which held her passion, Catherine spared no expense in the attempt to achieve her goals. She recruited leading economists, such as Arthur Young and Jacques Necker, to become foreign members of her Free Economic Society, which she established to help modernize the Russian economy. She brought leading scientists of the day, including Leonhard Euler, a Swiss mathematician, physicist, astronomer, logician, and engineer who made important contributions to topology and analytic number theory, and zoologist and botanist Peter Simon Pallas to teach in the Russian Academy of Sciences in St. Petersburg. The academy had ample financial resources from the government and emphasized research in pursuing scientific questions and improving Russian education. Catherine also recruited Anders Johan

Lexell to the academy. Lexell was a Finnish-Swedish astronomer, mathematician, and physicist, and he was one of the most prolific members of the academy, publishing 66 papers in 16 years, and making significant contributions in the fields of polygonometry and celestial mechanics. For the latter, a comet was named in his honor.

Another area of Catherine's passion was philosophy. She actively endeavored to incorporate principles of the Enlightenment she learned from studying the works of French philosophers into her legislation. She openly admitted taking from the works of, most notably, Montesquieu and Cesare Beccaria when she prepared "Instructions for the Guidance of the Assembly," which was intended for the Grand Commission she created as a type of consultative parliament. The 652-member commission was tasked with considering the needs of the Russian Empire and suggesting means to satisfy those needs. The commission never evolved beyond the realm of theory, but that didn't stop Catherine from issuing codes to address some of the modernization trends in her *Nakaz*, a set of legal principles compiled as a guide for the replacement of the mid-seventeenth-century Muscovite code of laws. Among these principles was the equality of all men before the law and a stated disapproval of the death penalty and torture, some of the very same principles later incorporated into both the United States Constitution and the Polish Constitution. While Catherine espoused these principles, they frightened many of her more moderate advisors, and for this reason, she held off putting them into practice immediately.

Catherine did put into practice statutes that would increase the Russian population. Among these was the Statute for the Administration of the Provinces of the Russian Empire which sought to divide the country into provinces and districts as well as increase the population. Fifty provinces and nearly 500 districts were created with this statute, and this required the appointment of more than double the government officials, who then spent nearly six times as much on local government. While Catherine increased the power of the nobles by organizing them in their efforts to bring their concerns to the monarch, she also limited their power by creating a Charter of Towns, which divided all people into six groups, thereby effectively creating what could be viewed as a middle estate—an entity somewhat similar to a middle class—among nobility.

Finally, in her efforts to modernize Russian culture, she issued a number of legal innovations. She described these to Voltaire as moving Russia in a more modern direction, "little by little." These included the Code of Commercial Navigation and Salt Trade Code of 1781, the Police Ordinance of 1782, and the Statute of National Education of 1786, which as discussed earlier, established the two-tier national educational system.

Another means by which Catherine sought to increase the Russian population was by extending the borders of the Russian Empire. Toward this end, she pursued diplomacy when possible and warfare when that failed.

Chapter Four

Catherine the Warrior

"I sincerely want peace, not because I lack resources for war, but because I hate bloodshed."

—Catherine the Great

Catherine's goal for extending the borders of the Russian Empire was to move southward and westward by absorbing New Russia, Crimea, Northern Caucasus, Right-bank Ukraine, Belarus, Lithuania, and Courland. This would take place mostly through conflict with two powers: the Ottoman Empire and the Polish-Lithuanian Commonwealth. Prior to the start of conflicts, she agreed to a commercial treaty with Great Britain in 1766. She saw the benefits of an alliance with Britain, but she stopped short of a full military alliance as she was wary of threatening the European balance of power by further increasing Britain's authority.

Catherine began her accession of territory by completing the conquest of the south, on the edge of the Black Sea. Peter had gained a toehold in this region, and Catherine completed what he had begun. She handed the Ottoman Empire some of its worst defeats in Turkish history in the conflict known as the first Russo-Turkish War, which lasted from 1768-1774. One of the Russian victories was the Battle of Chesme, which is located in the area between the western tip of Anatolia and the island of Chios. There, the Russian Navy bombarded the Ottoman ships and land positions on July 6, 1770. This battle resulted in the loss of almost the entire Ottoman fleet of ships, and it was the greatest naval defeat the Ottomans ever suffered. It gave the Russians control of the Aegean Sea for quite some time, and the defeat speeded up the rebellion of a number of minority groups in the Ottoman Empire, notable among them the Orthodox Christian nations in the Balkans.

The second battle of significance was that of the Battle of Kagul. This was not only one of the most important land battles in this conflict, but it was also one of the largest battles of the eighteenth century. It was fought on July 21, 1770, in Moldavia near the village of Frumoasa (which is now Cahul, Moldova). Here, some 40,000 Russian soldiers confronted the allied forces of the Ottoman Empire and the Khanate of Crimea, which totaled over 80,000 soldiers and infantrymen. Despite the inequality in the sizes of the forces, the Russians suffered only 1,000 casualties as compared with the 20,000 casualties on the Ottoman side.

Russia's eventual victory in the conflict resulted in the acquisition of what is now southern Ukraine as well as a small strip of the Black Sea coast between the Dnieper and Bug Rivers. Russia also gained access to the territories of Azov, Kerch, Yenikale, and Kinburn, and restrictions were lifted on Russian naval or commercial traffic in the Azov Sea. Russia also became the protector of Orthodox

Christians in the Ottoman Empire, and Crimea became a protectorate as well. Catherine later annexed the Crimea, and after the second Russo-Turkish War, the Russian claim to Crimea was legitimized. Fought between 1787 and 1792, this conflict involved an unsuccessful attempt by the Ottoman Empire to regain some of the land lost during the first war. Though Russia was largely successful in the battles waged during the conflict, Catherine was wary of Prussia entering the war, and after defeating the Ottomans at Machin, both countries agreed to a truce on July 21, 1791. The treaty legitimized Russia's claim to the Crimea, and also gave Russia the Yedisan region.

Catherine again waged war, this time against Persia, in 1796. She went to war after Persia invaded Georgia in 1795. In 1783, Russia had signed the Treaty of Georgievsk where it agreed to protect the Georgians against any new invasion from Persia. Thus, when Agha Mohammad Khan invaded Georgia in 1795, established rule over it, and expelled newly formed Russian garrisons, Catherine was obligated to act. Catherine had followed the advice of her lover, Prince Zubov, and put his younger brother, Count Valerian Zubov, in control of her forces rather than a seasoned general. Zubov began by storming the fortress of Derbent on May 10, and following success there, he continued through what is modern-day Azerbaijan, taking three principal cities—Baku, Shemakha, and Ganja. By November, they were in a position to attack mainland Iran.

The empress had praised the rapid progress Zubov had made to that point, but she would not be there to see the battle end. Catherine would suddenly die and her son, Paul, who succeeded her, had other plans for the raging conflict and ordered the troops to return to Russia. That angered the powerful Zubov family, and many of them were among the conspirators involved Paul's assassination five years later.

Catherine also fought a brief war against Sweden from 1788-1790. The conflict was instigated by King Gustav III of Sweden, who was Catherine's cousin. Gustav initiated the conflict in part to distract attention from political problems he was having at home, and also, he needed to win a war in order to fulfill his role as a successful and powerful monarch. Gustav expected to be able to overtake the Russian forces as they were still engaged in fighting with the Ottoman Empire, and from there, he had planned to attack St. Petersburg directly.

Russia's Baltic Fleet, however, engaged the Royal Swedish Navy in the Battle of Hogland, a conflict which neither side won, but the Swedish Army failed to advance, and subsequently, Denmark declared war on Sweden in 1788 in what is known as the Theatre War. Russia was, at that time, determined to defeat Sweden, but in July 1789, the Swedish Navy overpowered the Russian Navy at the Battle of Svensksund. The loss forced the Russians to the negotiating table, and in 1790, both parties signed the Treaty of Värälä. The treaty returned all conquered territories to their original owners and confirmed the Treaty of Åbo that resulted in Russian control of the southern part of Karelia.

Finally, Catherine waged another war with Poland, the Polish-Russian War of 1792. It was even shorter, having been fought between May and July of 1792. Catherine rejected many of the principles of Enlightenment she had once promoted after the French Revolution of 1789. She was fearful that resurgence of power after the May Constitution of 1791 would eventually threaten the monarchy in Russia and many other European countries.

The Constitution of May, as it is also known, sought to establish a more democratic constitutional monarchy in the Polish-Lithuanian Commonwealth. It established some elements of political equality between Polish townspeople and the nobility, and it gave peasants the protection of the government, thereby mitigating the worst abuses perpetrated by the nobility on serfs. Catherine, therefore, decided to intervene. In the conflict, Russia, with over 30,000 more soldiers, quickly defeated Polish forces in Lithuania and Ukraine, but over the course of the three-month war, no one scored a decisive victory. The Polish forces only managed one victory over a Russian formation at the Battle of Zieleńce on June 18, but faced with extended battle, the Polish King Stanislaw August Poniatowski decided to ask for a ceasefire. With this victory as well as victory in the Kościuszko Uprising in 1794, Russia was able to complete the partitioning of Poland wherein all remaining territory was divided between Prussia and Austria in 1795.

While Catherine was not afraid to wage war, it was not the only tool at her disposal. She also believed very firmly in diplomacy, and she strongly desired to be recognized as an enlightened sovereign. She established Russia in the role of international mediator, a role that Britain would later play in the nineteenth and twentieth centuries. She mediated the War of the Bavarian Succession fought in 1778 and 1779 between the German states of Prussia and Austria, and she established the League of Armed Neutrality in 1780 to defend shipping by neutral interests from the British Royal Navy during the American Revolution. She also attempted to establish open trade relations with Japan, even sending a government dispatched trade mission there in 1792. This was prompted by Russian government assistance of a Japanese sea captain, Daikokuya Kodayu, whose ship ran ashore in the Aleutian Islands, which were part of Russia at that time. Russian authorities helped the captain and his crew, and in return, he acted as a trade envoy. The Japanese government subsequently received the trade mission sent by Russia, but the negotiations ultimately failed.

Despite some failures, Catherine's actions taken as commander of her armed forces reflect a nuanced understanding of political and military strategies common to the time period. As with her desire to become ruler, she took the time to understand the underlying politics of conflict and the military strategies required to achieve her goals.

Chapter Five

Catherine's Personal Life and Death

"Men make love more intensely at 20, but make love better, however, at 30."

—Catherine the Great

Upon meeting Catherine the Great, Madame Vigée Le Brun, the former court painter to Marie Antoinette, described her as follows in her memoirs:

"The sight of this famous woman so impressed me that I found it impossible to think of anything: I could only stare at her. Firstly, I was very surprised at her small stature; I had imagined her to be very tall, as great as her fame. She was also very fat, but her face was still beautiful, and she wore her white hair up, framing it perfectly. Her genius seemed to rest on her forehead, which was both high and wide. Her eyes were soft and sensitive, her nose quite Greek, her colour high and her features expressive. She addressed me immediately in a voice full of sweetness, if a little throaty: 'I am delighted to welcome you here, Madame, your reputation runs before you.'"

While Catherine's impressive appearance gave her an aura of power, few described her as beautiful. Still, she attracted many lovers over the course of her reign. She had detested her husband, marrying him only to achieve her goal of becoming empress. Once rid of him, she never again remarried. She did, however, take many lovers, keeping them only as long as they held her interest, and for Catherine the Great, that meant more than physical beauty.

Catherine often elevated her lovers to high positions, and when the affair was over, she would pension them with gifts of serfs and large estates. Her lovers often returned her kindness toward them even after the relationship had ended. When her affair with Grigori Aleksandrovich Potemkin ended in 1776, he is said to have selected a replacement lover for Catherine whom he felt had the physical beauty and mental agility to hold her interest. Her generosity toward her lovers was legendary. Pyotr Zavadovsky reportedly received 50,000 rubles, a pension of 5,000 rubles, and 4,000 peasants after she ended their affair in 1777. Her last lover was Prince Zubov, and he was 40 years her junior. Her sexual independence was unusual for the time, and it spawned many legends about her.

Catherine's first lover was the Count Sergei Vasilievich Saltykov, a Russian military officer. He became her lover shortly after her arrival in Russia. In her memoirs, she implies that he was the father of her son, Paul I of Russia. Some dispute that fact, noting that Paul strongly resembled Peter III in both character and physical appearance. Saltykov was described as tall and handsome while Paul was pugnacious and stocky;

however, in her memoirs, Catherine discussed the ugliness of Saltykov's brother and suggested Saltykov was the father.

She took another lover when she was 26 years old, after a decade of marriage to the then-Grand Duke Peter. His name was Stanislaw Poniatowski, and he had been offered a place in the British embassy for gaining her as an ally. Catherine bore him a daughter named Anna Petrovna in December 1757, who sadly, as mentioned before, died at only four months of age. In 1763, Catherine supported Poniatowski as a candidate for the next king of Poland after the death of King Augustus III. When Frederick II warned her against trying to conquer Poland by marrying Poniatowski, something which all of Europe would oppose, Catherine responded that she had no intention of marrying him and she told him to marry someone else to remove suspicion of that. He refused to do so.

By that time, Catherine had already given birth to Orlov's child. Grigory Orlov was the grandson of a rebel who fought against Peter the Great. He opposed Peter's pro-Prussian sentiments, something with which Catherine disagreed. By 1759, she and Orlov were lovers. He was instrumental in the coup against her husband, but she refused to marry him after she was crowned Empress of Russia. While she found Grigory useful, Catherine came to believe he was inept at politics and she subsequently found his advice useless. When she dismissed him, she rewarded him with a palace in St. Petersburg, and she also gave him and his brothers titles, money, swords, and other gifts. She bore him a son, Aleksey Grigorievich Bobrinsky, before her ascension to the throne. The boy was raised in a village in Tula Guberniya called Bobriki, and Catherine sent him a letter avowing her maternity in 1781. His half-brother Paul would make him Count of the Russian Empire and promote him to general-major on the fifth day of his reign. Aleksey married a baroness, and many of his children and grandchildren went on to be successful in business, politics, and science. His son, Count Aleksey Alexandrovich was active in science as a historian and noted archaeologist. He was, in fact, named Chairman of the Imperial Archaeological Commission in 1886. He was also Vice-President of the Academy of Arts and Chairman of the Free Economic Society in 1894.

Another of Catherine's lovers, as mentioned above, was Prince Grigori Potemkin, whom some have claimed was her morganatic husband. A morganatic marriage is one between an individual of higher rank with one of lower rank. In this type of marriage, the passage of titles and privileges of the higher rank individual are prevented.

In total, Catherine was said to have taken 22 male lovers over the course of her life. Many benefitted financially and politically from their liaisons with her, and many were significantly younger than her. She also collected erotic furniture. She kept an erotic cabinet adjacent to her suite of rooms in Gatchina, which was the administrative center of Gatchinsky District in Leningrad Oblast, approximately 28 miles (45 kilometres) south of St. Petersburg. The cabinet reportedly contained highly eccentric furniture such as tables with large penises for legs and other furniture with penises and vulvas carved in relief. Erotic art decorated the walls, and artifacts from Pompeii augmented the collection. There were also statues of a naked man and a naked woman in the cabinet. Photographs exist of the room, but Russian authorities have been very secretive about it. The room and furniture were last seen in 1941 by Wehrmacht officers, but after that, they disappeared.

Catherine is also said to have used the Countess Praskovya Bruce as a "L'éprouveuse," or "tester of male capacity." In this role, every potential lover first spent a night with Praskovya before becoming Catherine's lover. The friendship was cut short, however, when Praskovya was found with Catherine's youthful lover, Rimsky-Korsakov.

In the memoirs published by French author Charles François Philibert Masson, entitled *Secret Memoirs of the Court of St. Petersburg*, Masson wrote that Catherine had "two passions, which never left her but with her last breath: the love of man, which degenerated into licentiousness, and the love of glory, which sunk into vanity. By the first of these passions, she was never so far governed as to become a Messalina, but she often disgraced both her rank and sex: by the second, she was led to undertake many laudable projects, which were seldom completed, and to engage in unjust wars, from which she derived at least that kind of fame which never fails to accompany success."

As passionate and successful as Catherine's life was, as she neared death, she faced two failures. She had hoped to make her granddaughter Queen of Sweden by marriage to King Gustav IV Adolph. She hosted a ball designed to announce their engagement, but Gustav, though quite taken with Alexandra, was bothered by the fact that she would not convert to Lutheranism, and he refused to appear at the ball. Catherine fell ill as a result of her irritation at this stunt. She recovered, and then planned a ceremony to announce that her favorite grandson would succeed her rather than her son, Paul. But these plans were not meant to be, and she would die before she could make the announcement.

On November 16, 1796, Catherine began her work day after what she described as a particularly good night's sleep. Sometime after 9:00 in the morning, she collapsed from a stroke while on the toilet. She was found sprawled on the floor, with a purplish appearance and weak pulse, by her attendant, Zakhar Zotov. The servants lifted her and brought her to her bed where, some 45 minutes later, her physician, Dr. John Rogerson, determined she had suffered a stroke. Catherine fell into a coma and never recovered. After being given last rites, she died the following evening around 9:45 pm. She was 67 years old.

An autopsy confirmed the cause of death as stroke, though later, unfounded stories would circulate regarding her death. One held that she died after attempting to engage in sexual relations with a horse. In this version, she was reportedly crushed to death when the harness holding the horse above her broke. Another story alleged she was assassinated by blades that sprung from the toilet seat. However, none of these alternative versions of her death are substantiated by any reasonable evidence.

Catherine's will gave specific instructions for her burial. She was to be dressed in white with a golden crown on her head. She wanted the crown inscribed with her Christian name. She also stated that the mourning period should last no longer than six months, and that shorter was better. Despite the provisions of her will, she was buried in a silver brocade dress, but she did have a gold crown on her head. Her coffin was richly decorated in gold fabric, and it was placed on a platform at the Grand Gallery's chamber of mourning. For six weeks, her body lay in state and was kept lit day and night. She was buried at the Peter and Paul Cathedral in St. Petersburg.

Catherine's son, Paul, succeeded her to the throne, though he would be assassinated only five years after doing so. His son, the favorite grandson that Catherine had wanted to replace her, Alexander, succeeded him. Alexander I declined to punish the assassins who had taken his father's life.

Conclusion

Catherine the Great's life could be described as both ambitious and eccentric. She focused her efforts on rising to the role of Empress of Russia, and she was wildly successful in that endeavor, particularly given that she was not Russian by birth. Despite this, she is thought of as one of Russia's greatest rulers. She presided over the Russian Golden Age of Enlightenment, and she promoted the principles of the European Enlightenment.

During her reign, she undertook the enormous task of reforming the Russian education system, something she sought to do in accordance with modern European educational theories that focused on both morality and academic education. She also sought to modernize the Russian culture, including the arts, sciences, and economy, which she felt were woefully backward in principle and practice. Toward that end, she spared no expense. Her actions, even those that ended ultimately in failure, laid the foundation for future leaders to build upon.

As a warrior, she comported herself well. The wars fought during her reign were largely successful in achieving the goals she set. These included expanding the Russian Empire and building its population. Russians, even Soviet Russians, largely admire her. Though they see her as a German usurper and profligate, they still consider her to be a source of national pride. Under her rule, Russia grew strong enough to threaten other great powers, and she is one of few women rulers to have had their names become synonymous with a decisive epoch in the development of their country.

By the end of her reign, Russia had expanded to an area of more than 200,000 square miles. Additionally, Catherine had brought the ancient Russian rulers' dream of access to the Bosporus Strait within reach as a result of her territorial expansion. Catherine, herself, claimed to have reorganized 29 provinces under her reform plan, and she built more than 100 new towns as well as expanded and renovated many more. These achievements, along with her military victories, and the fame of her brilliant court to which she drew some of the greatest minds in Europe, won her a distinguished place in not only Russian history but world history as well.

Her critics, while acknowledging her abilities, point out that many of her achievements were due to the talents of her associates, and she ultimately failed to achieve many of the long-term goals she sought to accomplish. This is, perhaps, an unfair judgment given that many leaders rely heavily on advisors, and of course, one measure of success is based on the successful people with whom one chooses to associate. It seems unlikely that modern leaders would fault her for associating with the brilliant minds of her day.

Critics also judge her personal life harshly. She devoted her life to power above all else, and this at the expense of her dreams of the joys of a shared love. She did not love the husband she married, nor her son Paul, who was recognized as the legitimate heir to the throne. She was alleged to have been complicit in the assassination of her husband, whom she despised. She also stated that all three of the children she bore were illegitimate. Catherine has been variously described as promiscuous, vain, egotistical, pretentious, and power-hungry.

On the other hand, she was a generous lover—even after the affair ended. She was also a loyal correspondent who counted the likes of Voltaire and Denis Diderot among the friends with whom she regularly corresponded. An established writer, an able philosopher, and an avid collector of art, Catherine was intellectually curious and a capable military strategist. The fact that she relied on the wisdom, experience, and knowledge of the capable advisors she drew to her court speaks volumes about her character. While she likely would not have referred to herself in this manner, Catherine was, in fact, an early feminist. She promoted the co-education of girls in Russia and created the famed Smolny Institute toward that end.

As the longest-ruling empress in history, she is one of the most remarkable Russian rulers of either sex. The principles she promoted and instituted during her reign not only shaped the future of Russia but the world as well. Regardless of whether she is viewed harshly or heroically, her legacy will undoubtedly endure.

Made in the USA
Las Vegas, NV
09 April 2024

88478298R00024